TRANS... YESTERDAY AND TODAY

by Coco Relf

illustrated by John Hovell

Orlando   Boston   Dallas   Chicago   San Diego

Visit *The Learning Site!*

www.harcourtschool.com

Travel by Foot

Long, long ago, people had one way to get around. They walked. A person can walk only about four miles an hour, so people stayed close to home. They ate what grew around them and what they could catch.

The ancient Romans, though, had a huge amount of land. To send messages they had runners who took news from place to place. Often, one man would start. Another man would wait for him on the trail, grab the message, and run with it further. The fastest men could run about 60 miles a day.

Using Animals to Travel

Thousands of years ago, people in Europe saw how fast horses ran. They began taming and riding the horses. That way, they could go much faster than by walking. A horse can run up to 70 miles an hour (but not for very long).

In Asia, people used camels, which can travel long distances in the desert and eat very little. Camels are not all that fast. Their fastest move is a trot of about four to eight miles an hour. On the other hand, they can carry a lot.

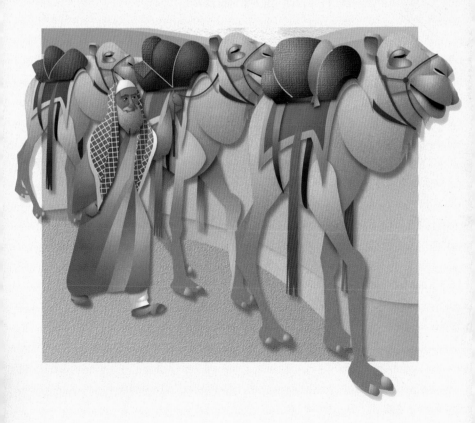

Once people thought up the wheel, the cart came next. Sometimes people pulled carts, but horses did a much better job. Horses could pull carts with people and their luggage. Carts could travel only as fast as trotting horses. Having the horse do the work was still helpful.

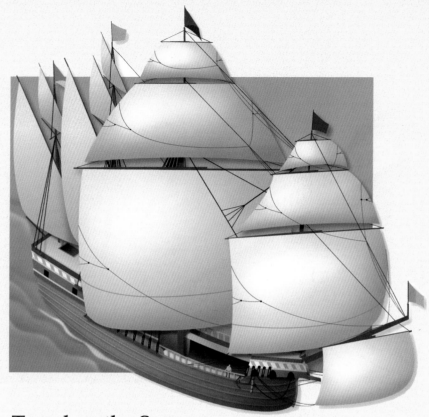

Travel on the Sea

Ships are another very old way to travel. People rowed the first ships. Then they started using sails. Ships began to travel on the oceans of the world. By the middle of the 1500s, sailing ships had up to 35 sails. They could travel 23 miles an hour with a good wind.

Sailing ships had one big problem. If there was no wind, the ship didn't move. In the 1800s, ships powered by steam engines changed ocean travel. In the 1500s, an ocean trip by ship might take three months. On one of the new sturdy steamships, the trip would take 20 days.

Travel on Land

Also in the 1800s, people on land were
building train tracks. Steam engines,
moved the trains at new high speeds. By
the late 1800s, some trains in Europe could
go as fast as 60 miles an hour.

There were no trains for people going to California in the mid 1800s. Families went west with huge wagons. They walked because there was little space in the wagons. The trips were long, too. The wagons could travel only at about two miles an hour.

In the early 1900s, most people in this country traveled in carriages pulled by horses. Not many people took long trips. Traveling by horse and buggy took too long. If your relatives or friends moved far away, you might not see them for years.

In 1908, Henry Ford started building his Model T cars which changed the world. The cars did not cost much, so Ford sold millions of them. These cars could go pretty fast–up to 45 miles an hour. Then good roads were needed.

Taking to the Sky

People have always wanted to travel by air. Hot-air balloons have been used to carry people since 1783. Balloons can go as fast as 30 miles an hour.

Before Ford sold his Model T, two brothers created flying machines that used engines. The Wright brothers flew their first airplane that worked in 1903.

By the 1930s, some people traveled on small planes at up to 170 miles an hour. Today, you can sit back in a plane and listen to a cassette or chat with companions. The jet you are sitting in roars across the sky at 500 miles an hour.

The men and women on the space shuttle go even faster. They fly at more than 17,000 miles an hour! At that rate, it takes ten minutes to travel between New York and Los Angeles.

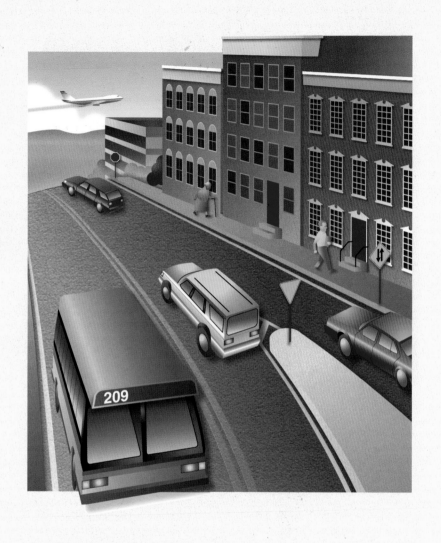

People can now travel in many different ways. We still walk, but we can go so much faster.